Spot The Tick...
in England

by

Lorraine Damonte

Grosvenor House
Publishing Limited

All rights reserved
Copyright © Lorraine Damonte, 2017

The right of Lorraine Damonte to be identified as the author of this
work has been asserted by him in accordance with Section 78
of the Copyright, Designs and Patents Act 1988

The book cover picture is copyright to Lorraine Damonte

This book is published by
Grosvenor House Publishing Ltd
Link House
140 The Broadway, Tolworth, Surrey, KT6 7HT
www.grosvenorhousepublishing.co.uk

This book is sold subject to the conditions that it shall not, by way of
trade or otherwise, be lent, resold, hired out or otherwise circulated
without the author's or publisher's prior consent in any form of binding or
cover other than that in which it is published and
without a similar condition including this condition being imposed
on the subsequent purchaser.

A CIP record for this book
is available from the British Library

ISBN 978-1-78623-067-6

Acknowledgements

To my Mum, for her love and wisdom, for her encouragement and support through this journey called Lyme.

To the stars of my book, my daughters Nicole and Madeleine…I love you X

About the Author

The creator of this book is a not an artist or a writer but a mother of two girls.

Nicole being the eldest daughter, Madeleine is the youngest.

While painting the pictures, Lorraine became very unwell.

Her doctor tested her for Lyme disease, for which the result was positive.

Other co-infections were discovered along with a heavy metal overload.

For five years, Lorraine took high dose antibiotics in combinations, chelation therapy, Chinese cupping and is now currently using a Rife machine and infrared sauna.

Lorraine's wish is to stop the suffering and make the public aware that the illness is real, and that you can take measures to prevent it.

About the book

The book explores mostly iconic London, the places and people to see while visiting England.

On each page there is a small tick to find, this is a fun way to bring awareness of small creatures that can transmit disease.

Lyme disease is a worldwide illness; it can be difficult to treat if not caught early. It is present across the UK. The sheep tick, the hedgehog tick, the fox tick; tick's also feed on deer, wild mammals and birds. Ticks can be found in the woods, fields, parks and gardens.

This is the first book to be published with the theme – Spot the Tick.

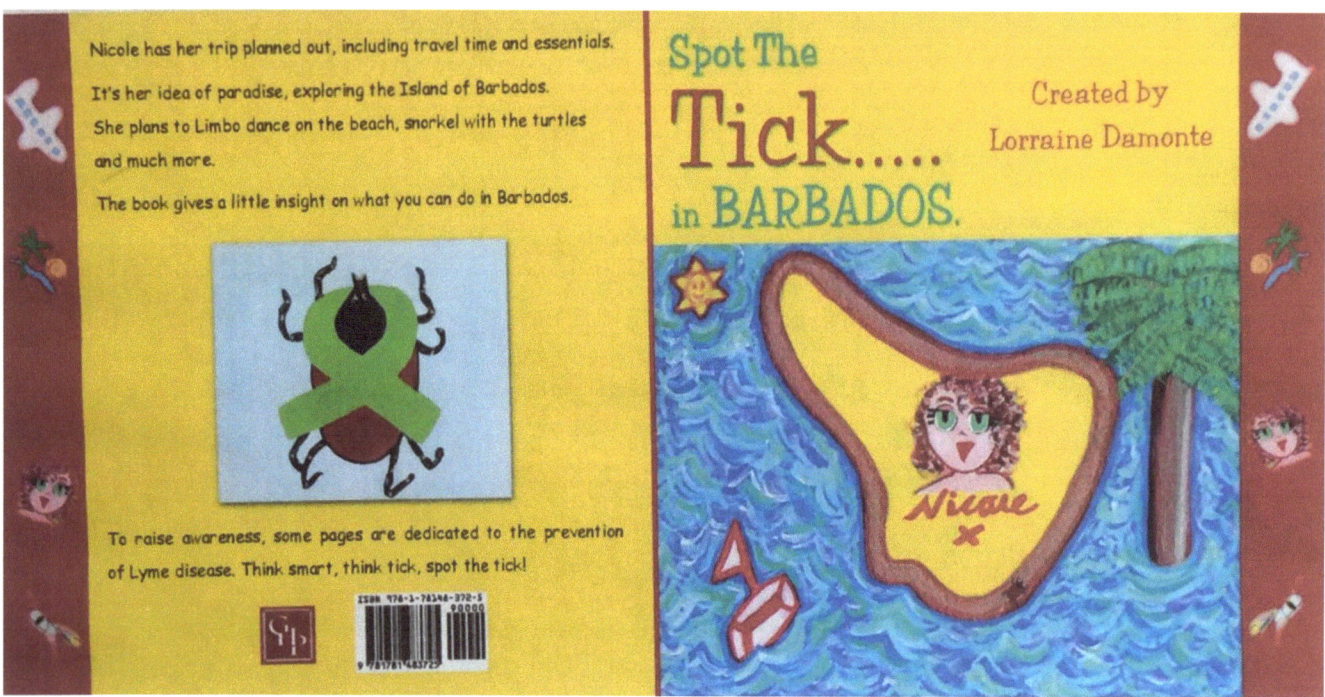

The ticks are placed in unlikely places just for fun.

There are pages dedicated to the prevention of Lyme disease at the back of the book.

Author's website
www.spotthetick.co.uk

SPOT THE TICK.....

IN ENGLAND.

Created by Lorraine Damonte

Hello, my name is Nicole.
and this is my little sister Madeleine.

We are going to England!

We are visiting England for a week away.

We are heading to the Eurotunnel, we shall drive all the way!

From Luxembourg, the drive will take four hours to Calais (France) 35 minutes to cross the English Channel, then an additional one and a half hours to the City of London. This in total will take approximately seven hours including waiting and boarding time.

On our arrival we will pass Big Ben.

We will check into a hotel and sleep until 10 am.

- *Big Ben is the nickname for the great bell of the clock, it dates back to 1859.*
- *It is officially known as The Elizabeth Tower.*
- *It was originally known as The Clock Tower and was renamed in 2012 to celebrate the Diamond Jubilee of Elizabeth II.*
- *Big Ben's timekeeping is regulated by a stack of coins placed on a huge pendulum.*

First on our 'to see' list is a visit to the Tower.

The Beefeaters on guard there are protecting the Crown Jewels by the hour.

- *The Crown Jewels are on display inside the Tower of London. They are estimated to be worth more than £20 billion. The Tower's Yeomen Warders were given the nickname Beefeaters from their daily ration of meat. The Tower dates back to the year 1066.*

Then it's on to see the Pearly King and Queen parading their attire for all to admire, while raising money for their dear charities.

We would like to give them our green ribbons and green buttons to wear, we too have our own cause that we would like to share 'Lyme disease awareness, think smart, think tick!'

Donations for research are needed with urgency, so let's work quick!

- *Their suits are decorated with pearl buttons, bold and shiny to attract attention, they were known as London's cockney 'Street Traders' and they date back 1,000 years.*

Next, it's on to the River Thames for a pleasure cruise extravaganza.

The drawbridge will rise as we pass through as though we are royalty!

• Tower Bridge is an iconic symbol of London, it dates back to 1886. Its upward swinging drawbridge provides clearance for large boats.

Next onto a London Double Decker bus to do some sightseeing from up high.

We will purchase a ticket so we can hop on and off when and if something catches our eye.

- 'Ding Ding' the bell on the bus would ring. 'All aboard' our great grandmother would call.

  She was a lady conductor in 1967. Today the driver works alone.

  London's iconic 'Routemaster' red buses first appeared in 1956.

Talking of eyes, we will visit the big one; it reaches clear into the sky.

Like a plane or a dove, flying high up above, we can see for 25 miles if we try.

- *The massive Ferris wheel was built in 1999; on a clear day you can see Windsor Castle.*
  It is already an iconic building, and is one of the tallest in the city of London.

To keep in touch with our mum and our chums, we will look out for the iconic red boxes.

A telephone call to say, 'We are fine, we are having a truly magnificent time!'

A postcard to say, 'Wish you were here,' and to promise to invite you along next year.

* Red telephone boxes are rare today as most people carry a mobile phone. Some of the boxes are restored and sold for antique garden ornaments.

Lunchtime will call and some traditional pub grub is what we have planned for our menu.

It's fish and chips for me, and bangers and mash for Maddie, following on with a nice cup of tea.

* *Indian food is now considered to be top for the British favourites, but traditionally it was fish and chips, sausage and mash, pie and mash or a Sunday roast.*

Our most important day planned, is to visit the Queen of England; most grand.

Through the crowds we will wave and cheer, 'Long live the Queen!' If we are lucky she will catch our eye, smile and give us her royal wave.

- *Queen Elizabeth II is the longest serving monarch. She lives and works in Buckingham Palace, but she considers her home to be Windsor Castle.*

We will then leave the city and on to the North, as there is a famous forest to see, do you know the story of Robin Hood?

Robin Hood lived here...

with his merry men

We plan to picnic under his tree!

- *The Major Oak can be found in Sherwood Forest.*
- *It was voted Britain's favourite tree and is between 800–1,000 years old.*

For Saint George's day, we will surely play castles, knights and dragons!

Tamworth Castle is the place to visit for a medieval feast of fun!

- *Saint George is England's patriot saint. The hero of the Golden Legend.*
- *It is said the hero slayed a dragon to save the life of a princess and then he gave the town access to fresh water. The people converted to Christianity to give thanks for his bravery.*
- *This day falls on the 23rd April.*

Maypole dancing is a traditional dance, to celebrate the coming of summer.

Ribbons entwine, music and dance, singing so sweet to the ear, then one lucky girl will be chosen and crowned as the most beautiful Queen of the Year. The May Day Queen!

- *May Day is the 1st of May. It's a traditional spring holiday. King Charles II erected a maypole in London's Strand to signal fun times; it stood there for fifty years.*

The last day of sightseeing, a coach tour to Wiltshire is what we have in store, Stonehenge is a place of mystery and magic we simply will adore.

An ancient circle of stones is what we will find there, what is its purpose? "It's a clock", astronomers declare.

- *It was somehow used to track the sun and the moon's movements and was used as a solar calendar. It was built around 4,000 to 5,000 years ago.*

Before we head home, it's down to the Den. Junior lions are we! One lucky Lion has an incredible time warming up and leading out the team!

* *Football dates back to medieval times. It has been said that on Christmas Day 1915 during World War 1, the British soldiers got out of the trenches and played football with the Germans.*

   Lions represent the players and the supporters, as a treat a child gets to warm up and lead the players into the stadium.

We are going to England!

It's going to be fun!

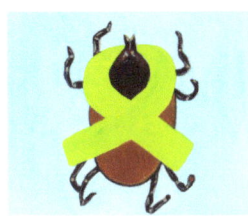

Lyme Disease Awareness & Support

It must be noted that Lyme infected ticks can be found in grassy and wooded areas anywhere in the UK.

For up to date information and patient support please visit the following charities.

www.caudwelllyme.com

www.lymediseaseuk.com

Awareness packs for schools and children are available.

Beware of the tick he is looking for lunch, he can be so tiny, as small as a poppy seed.

Ticks like to hang out in these places:

When going into the woods, wear light coloured long sleeved clothing, tuck trousers into socks, tie hair back and wear a hat.

Spray Mosi-guard Natural over your skin and clothes for protection against biting insects.   www.mosi-guard.com

Check all areas of the body for ticks, are there any unusual freckles? Ask a parent to help with difficult to see places.

Remove tick within 24 hours with fine tipped tweezers, or a tick remover. Do not twist and pull upwards

- *Warning, there is no evidence to prove transmission time, it could be immediate. A tick can feed up to seven days before dropping off.*

Place tick into a container and store, the tick can be tested for bacteria should a person become ill.

It is possible to take a tick to the vets, for a charge they can screen the tick for bacteria.

Place outerwear like coats into a tumble dryer on a hot setting to kill any hidden ticks.

A gorgeous pretty deer in the woods we can see… is he carrying ticks? Yes indeed.

Sheep, hedgehog, fox and deer ticks feed on wild mammals and birds.

Important information for parents

Early Lyme disease symptoms:

A bull's-eye rash: usually appearing between two to 30 days of being bitten.

Warning: One in three people report not seeing a rash.

Flu like symptoms: Tiredness, muscle pain, fever, joint pains, tendon pain, chills, stiff neck.

Bell's palsy: face drops on one side.

Nerve pains: sharp shocks.

Eye: disturbances and pain.

Tummy: digestive upset.

Hearing: pain and dizziness.

Tick Attached:

If possible go to the nearest hospital to have the tick removed.

Ask the nurse to place the tick into a secure plastic container. This you can take to a vet for screening to identify any infections.

Visit your doctor and ask for three weeks of antibiotics for tick attachment and possible Lyme disease exposure.

If you develop the above symptoms ask your GP for another three weeks of antibiotics.

The medical guidelines recommend three to six weeks.

The Lyme disease life cycle is described as being between three and 30 days long, so six weeks of antibiotics would be preferable. It is also advisable to continue with treatment until a person is symptom free.

Lyme disease is treatable with antibiotics, the sooner treatment begins the better the outcome.

Late Lyme disease symptoms: this can happen within three months of the bite.

Meningitis.

Encephalopathy/brain fog.

Encephalomyelitis/seizures/movement disorder.

Pain.

Swelling in joints including jaw, Lyme arthritis.

Bell's palsy.

Sensitivity to light, touch, sound or taste.

Heart problems.

Memory loss.

Severe cramping in calves, thighs and back with loss of muscle tone.

Other organ problems: liver, lung, gastrointestinal infection, spleen, bladder, kidney, thyroid and brain.

Electric shocks, crawling, shooting, tingling sensations.

Depression, anxiety, panic attacks.

Muscle twitching, tremor.

Weakness leading to paralysis.

Disturbed sleep, nightmares.

Dizziness, hearing loss and tinnitus.

Lyme associated stroke.

Lyme disease is caused by a bacteria called Borrelia burgdorferi: it is very clever and can change shape, evading the immune system.

Late Lyme disease would need a combination of antibiotics to kill each form: the spirochetes, the L-shaped (without a cell wall) and the cyst. The treatment plan can take years and be very costly.

Ticks can also carry other infections, which can complicate the diagnosis and treatment.

Therefore if the above symptoms are present, a Lyme literate doctor can check for co-infections too.

Recommended Blood tests: Western Blot, Elispot LTT and a CD57. Please note that the Elisa test as a screening tool is useless according to current research.

Message from the author

I hope you have enjoyed reading this book and are now aware of what to do should you be bitten by a tick.

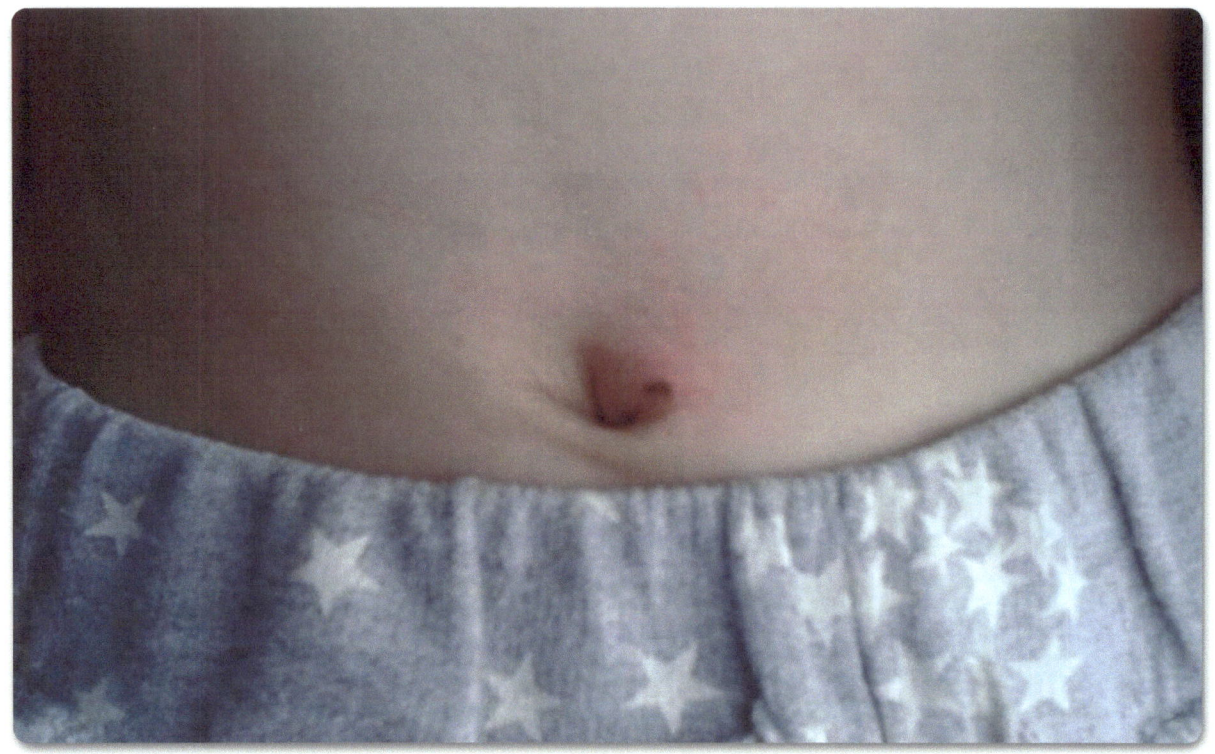

Madeleine was bitten by a deer tick on the 20th May 2016, she received in total four weeks of Clarithromycin.

She has since been well, her symptoms resolved.

www.ingramcontent.com/pod-product-compliance
Lightning Source LLC
Chambersburg PA
CBHW041537040426
42446CB00002B/130